LEGO Friends™

Friends to the Rescue!

Story and art by Blue Ocean

Friendship Fun written by Olivia London

Litt

LITTLE, BROWN BOOKS FOR YOUNG READERS

First published in the United States in 2016 by Little, Brown and Company
This edition published in Great Britain in 2016 by Hodder and Stoughton

1 3 5 7 9 10 8 6 4 2

LEGO, the LEGO logo, the FRIENDS logo, and the Brick and
Knob configurations are trademarks of the LEGO Group.

Produced by Hodder and Stoughton under license from the
LEGO Group. © 2016 The LEGO Group. All rights reserved.

Comic artwork © 2016 by Blue Ocean Entertainment AG, Germany
Stories written by Marisa Reinelt
Pencils and inks by Fernando Dominguez and Carlos Arroyo
Colors by Miriam Hidalgo and Oriol San Julian

A CIP catalogue record for this book
is available from the British Library.

ISBN 978-1-51020-060-9

Printed and bound in the United States

Little, Brown Books for Young Readers
An imprint of
Hachette Children's Group
Part of Hodder and Stoughton
Carmelite House
50 Victoria Embankment
London EC4Y 0DZ

An Hachette UK Company
www.hachette.co.uk

www.hachettechildrens.co.uk

Welcome to Heartlake City

Heartlake City is the home of LEGO
Friends, five very different and very
talented girls who are best friends. The
city is centered around a heart-shaped
lake (hence the name!), located directly
between a beach and a mountain range.
This location makes it perfect for all
kinds of outdoor activities like flying,
horseback riding, observing dolphins,
and more! The city is home to a mall,
a café, a bakery, a vet, a beauty shop,
a swimming pool, and so much more.

Great Places to Visit!

CLOVER MEADOWS
A place where people gather for picnics

CLEARSPRING MOUNTAINS
A mountain range with a spring

WHISPERING WOODS
A small forest in Heartlake City

MAIN STREET
A great place to hang out with your friends

HEARTLAKE STABLES
The horse stables that make up Summer Riding Camp

LAKE HEART
The heart-shaped lake in the center of the city, where people go to swim, fish, and ice-skate

THE PARK
The Heartlake Dog Show is held here.

HEARTLAKE HIGH

The local school attended by Andrea, Emma, Mia, Stephanie, and Olivia, and all their friends

THE BEACH

The coastline. Emma and Olivia live near here.

LIGHTHOUSE ISLAND

An island off the coast of Heartlake City

Andrea

The performer of the group, Andrea is a talented singer and is great at making up her own songs. She loves anything that relates to music: singing, playing the piano, dancing, and the theater. She is a great cook and works at a café. She also has a not-so-secret love of bunnies.

Emma

Emma is an artist and loves being creative. She enjoys interior design, taking photographs, and making jewelry. She's also a fan of horseback jumping and karate. She is sometimes forgetful, but she's a wonderful friend.

Mia

The animal lover of the group, Mia enjoys spending time with lots and lots of animals. If she's not training animals, then she's probably taking care of them. She also excels at sports, skateboarding, and playing the drums. In her free time, she rides horses, goes camping, and practices magic tricks.

Olivia

Olivia loves science, nature, and history. If she could, she would spend all day inventing new things, as well as taking pictures and drawing. Super intelligent and focused, Olivia is quite a brain. She's still clumsy sometimes, but who isn't?

Stephanie

A confident natural leader, Stephanie is very social, creative, and organized. She loves planning events, parties, and soccer. She enjoys talking to people, writing stories, and dancing ballet. Though at times a little bossy, she is very down-to-earth.

Oh Christmas Tree, Oh Christmas Tree!

In many households, December holidays are filled with joy, celebration, and lots of traditions. One of the most popular in Western cultures is decorating trees. Have you ever wondered where this tradition came from?

Decorating the home with branches from evergreen and fir trees can be traced back *thousands* of years. Ancient people celebrated the winter solstice (the shortest day of the year), as it marked the end of winter. To celebrate, people would decorate their homes with evergreen branches. These tree decorations served as reminders that summer was coming and helped people keep their spirits high during dark, cold days and nights. Yet, the best-known origin of the evergreen being used to celebrate Christmas—the way we know the tradition today—can be traced to Germany in the sixteenth century. Martin Luther, a devout Christian and popular religious reformer, was said to have been walking through a forest of evergreen trees when he noticed how magically the stars shone through the tree branches. He decided to cut down a tree, bring it home, and decorate it with candles to recreate the beauty for his family.

So how did this tradition come to America? In 1830, settlers from Germany came to Pennsylvania and displayed their Christmas trees, but this practice wasn't widely accepted among immigrants from other places. It wasn't until 1846, when Queen Victoria of England and her German husband, Prince Albert, were illustrated on the front cover of a British paper standing next to a beautifully decorated Christmas tree, that many British and Americans alike began to accept the Christmas tree as a part of the holiday tradition.

Now, the next time you see a Christmas tree, you'll know exactly where the idea came from! Share the story with a friend and see what other traditions there are and where they came from!

Something Completely Different!

AS THEY DO EVERY DAY, THE GIRLS ARE WALKING TO SCHOOL. BUT TODAY...

What's going on here? Why is everyone standing around outside?

We're supposed to take our class photos in front of the school statue tomorrow. Now everything is ruined!

Oh no! Who would do such a thing?!

Spray-painting graffiti all over Heartlake's most famous poet like that!

There goes our class photos.

But it's tradition to take them in front of the statue!

The Knitting Circle

Who knew that *knitting* could make such a huge difference to the Friends and their classmates? Using yarn and knitting needles, the Friends fixed a problem and made a positive change in their community. Have you ever thought about knitting?

In the past, some people believed that crafting hobbies like sewing or knitting were activities just for females. But in the last few decades, people of every age, gender, race, and class have begun picking up knitting needles. Some medical studies have revealed that knitting helps to reduce stress and sadness, and even strengthens the immune system! And of course, if you knit with your friends, then you can have a lot of laughs too.

But aside from these positive benefits, you can also use this hobby to address important issues all around you. Some people knit scarves and donate them to those less fortunate. Other people knit quilts for sale, using the proceeds to donate to their favorite charities. Knitting and knitting circles aren't silly—they can be an empowering and peaceful way to bring about social change!

Want to start your own knitting circle now? Go for it! Here are five quick tips to getting your own knitting circle off the ground:

LEARN

First, learn how to knit! It's not hard, but you may want to start by asking your friends and family if they know how. If they don't, ask your parents or guardian to take you to a local yarn or crafts store and sign up for a class!

INVITE

Ask your friends if they would like to be in your knitting circle. It's up to all of you if it's just for fun or for a special cause.

MEET

Once you have enough people, set a time and place for your first meeting. And don't forget the yarn! (Ask your parents first, of course—maybe they can make it a pizza party!)

DECIDE

Ask each person why they came and what they hope to get out of the group. Is there a particular problem or purpose that people want to address in their knitting? Or did they come just to make friends and knit? The group can be whatever you want it to be. (Remember, not everyone has to agree. If a few people want to work on one project but others want to do their own thing, that's okay too!)

HAVE FUN!

The main thing to remember about a knitting circle—whether it's for fun or for an important cause—is that it's made up of strong individuals who are friends first.

Top Ten Camping Tips

Have you ever wanted to go camping but were afraid to try because you've never done it before? Sure, new things can be scary, but doing them anyway has a funny way of making them not so scary. The more you know about something, the less likely you are to be nervous or afraid of it. The wilderness is a wonderful place, and even though nature is full of both good and bad things, there's nothing like being surrounded by a dome full of stars or falling asleep to the sounds of the natural world around you. They don't call it the great outdoors for nothing!

Follow these ten tips, and the next time your parents ask you to go camping, you won't want to wait to trade your bedroom for a tent!

Pack ONLY the Essentials

Depending on where you are camping and how

far your walk is, you'll need to decide what is essential and what is a luxury. If you are camping far away, remember that you will have to hike that distance with everything you need in your backpack—which someone has to carry! Go online and download a list of camping essentials and check off what you have and cross out what you won't need as you go along. But don't forget the important gadgets like a compass, a flashlight and batteries, and any tools you may need for opening your food packets.

Pick the Right Sleeping Bag

Sleeping bags are made in different ways for different seasons. If you go camping in the fall or winter, you'll need a sleeping bag that has a lower temperature rating—that means it will keep you warm when it gets cold at night. (Some places can get below 0 degrees!) Some fibers are lighter weight and therefore easier to carry, while others will dry faster, in case you encounter rain. Try to make the best choice based on when and where you are going.

Set Up Camp BEFORE Dark

Whether you are camping out under the stars, in a tent, or in an RV, always find the place you are sleeping for the night long before it gets too dark. That way, you have enough time and light to set up everything you'll need for the night ahead.

Know Your Poisonous Plants

Before you travel, be sure to study up on the most common poisonous plants in the camping area. Poison ivy, poison oak, and poison sumac are a few you should be able to spot, but there may be others that are indigenous to your specific hiking grounds—especially if you are going somewhere exotic. Take a small guidebook, snap pictures with your phone, or print out a cheat sheet with visuals so you can help decipher what is what in the wilderness.

Bug Spray! Bug Spray! Bug Spray!

It's a good idea to spray yourself with bug repellent, especially at night. You can also wear long sleeves and long pants when you sleep. This will keep your bites to a minimum. No itching for you!

Know Your Surroundings—Don't Get LOST!

If you have a map, study your camping grounds and the area you are hiking before you go. Being familiar with the names of different areas of the grounds will come in handy later on. Always bring a printed map with you. The GPS on your phone will help you until your phone runs out of battery life, then you'll be left without it. So, before you go, make sure you know how to read a map AND a compass, and bring both of them with you on your trip, just in case.

Pack HIGH PROTEIN and HIGH CARB Food

Camping is hard work, and you'll need energy to complete your hikes, make your camp, and enjoy any adventures you have along the way. Stock up on foods that are high in protein and keep well—like beef jerky, protein bars, drink powders, and trail mix.

Keep Clean

It's hard to stay as hygienic as you normally would when you are journeying into the great outdoors, but do your best to stay as clean as you can while out there. Use hand sanitizer before you eat or touch your face, and use fresh water streams to take mini baths when you can. Bring soap, toothpaste, a towel, and toilet paper with you. Bring a plastic bag to keep dirty clothes in, and one to keep your toiletries in so they don't get dirty or wet. The one thing you should NOT do is wear any perfume or cologne while you are camping—these scents will attract animals and bugs.

Bring a First-Aid Kit

A first-aid kit is ESSENTIAL. Yours should include the following: disinfectant cream or ointment, Band-Aids, gauze and/or bandages for blisters, sunscreen, spray or cream to sooth itchy bug bites, and water-purifying tablets.

WATER, WATER, and MORE WATER!

The absolute most important thing to remember when you go camping is that you must keep yourself hydrated. You should drink at least sixteen ounces of water every hour as long as you are doing any kind of strenuous activity or if you are exposed to the heat, even while in the shade. Drinking water will keep you feeling healthy and ready to tackle any adventure!

Stephanie Scores!

Women ROCK Soccer!

A Portrait of Mia Hamm

For female athletes, it can be tough to get recognition from the world—or even the people around you. Some people do not understand that a female can play just as hard as a male playing the same sport. In the US, women weren't even *allowed* to play professional soccer until the first women's league was established in 1951.

Today, there are plenty of talented, strong, and brave female athletes to admire. But only thanks to some very heroic women who stepped forward and helped change the world.

© Al Messerschmidt/Getty Images Sport/Getty Images

One of the most renowned female soccer players of all time is Mia Hamm. Born in 1972 in Alabama, Mia was the youngest female athlete to play for the US Women's National Team. And she was only fifteen years old! She played on her first soccer team when she was five, but she wasn't always quick on her feet. Mia was born with a foot condition that forced her to wear casts on her feet when she was a baby. But from the moment she got those off, she couldn't wait to use her legs.

When it was time to go to college, Mia went to the University of North Carolina, where she led her team to four NCAA Championships. In 1991, the US National Team won the World Cup—Mia was the youngest member ever to win, at only nineteen years old. She set a new record for the number of international goals scored: 108! She has scored a total of 149 international goals, which is more than any other female player. Mia has won three ESPY awards—one for Soccer Player of the Year. She was also chosen as the US Female Soccer Player of the Year five years in a row.

She has truly ROCKED the world of soccer and is still considered one of the best female players ever to have played the game of soccer.

Emma in a Jam

Wow, Stephanie! Your shirt is awesome!

Oh, thanks!

I made it myself. I love crafts!

Will you lend it to me so I can see how the sequins were sewn on?

Erm— well...

Please? I'll take really good care of it!

Oh, all right, then...

THEY QUICKLY EXCHANGE SHIRTS.

Great! You'll get it back tomorrow!

It's Strawberry Jam Time!

Your alarm clock just went off. It's 7:00 a.m., and you have to force yourself out of bed, into the shower, and downstairs before the bus comes for school. You could have the same old bowl of cereal and milk for breakfast like you do every day...*or* you could have a fresh batch of delicious strawberry jam from this AWESOME recipe! Try making it with your friends or family this weekend, and breakfast next week will taste like a dream. It won't actually be a dream—you'll still have to wake up and go to school. But it will make your morning a lot *sweeter*!

SAFETY FIRST!

Remember, accidents do happen from time to time, so it's always a good idea for an adult to help or supervise. They might even know a few fun cooking tricks of their own!

Ingredients:

- ✿ 1 pound strawberries
- ✿ ⅔ cup sugar
- ✿ 1 fresh lemon

What You'll Need:

- ✿ Canning jars to store the jam in
- ✿ A pot
- ✿ A stirring spoon

What to Do:

1. First, clean the jars and prepare them for canning by pouring boiling water into the jars and onto the lids (place the lids in a pan and cover them with water). Let them sit like this for at least five minutes. Once they are clean, pour the water out and turn the jars upside down on a cooling rack to dry.

2. Next, clean the strawberries and hull them (remove the green leaves and core of the fruit at the top). Cut them into quarters. Pour the strawberries into a large

© Monkey Business Images/Shutterstock.com

pot and then add the sugar. Stir the mixture and mash the strawberries a little to release their juice. Let this mixture sit for at least two hours.

3. After the mixture has sat at room temperature for a couple of hours, put it on the stove at medium-to-high heat for approximately 10–15 minutes, stirring occasionally, until the jam thickens. Remove any foam that floats to the surface as the strawberries cook.

4. Squeeze in the lemon juice and bring the mixture to a boil. Then lower the heat and continue to stir. Check the consistency of your jam by spooning a little out and placing the spoon in the  freezer for a minute. When you remove it, if the consistency is to your liking, the jam is done. If you want it to be thicker, keep cooking a little longer, but don't let it sit on the heat too long.

© kostasgr/Shutterstock.com

5. Pour the jam into the jars, close your jars (or seal with a canning technique if you need to), and refrigerate. And don't forget to eat up—and enjoy!

SHARING IS CARING! Remember, homemade jellies and jams are a wonderful gift for anyone!

© gkrphoto/Shutterstock.com

Foaling in Love

Hey! Is it here yet?

pant

No, no. Take it easy. You haven't missed anything!

I'm sooo excited about Sunshine's baby foal. I just can't wait for it to come!

Yes, it could arrive any day now.

I'm not going to leave you alone until the foal has arrived!

OLIVIA KEEPS HER PROMISE AND STAYS THE WHOLE DAY.

YAAAAAWN

Boy, am I tired! I'll just take a quick nap...

58

It Runs in the Family

Horses are beautiful and intelligent creatures. In many cultures, they are seen as heroic, majestic animals. The scientific name for the horse is *Equus*, which is why you may have heard the term *equine* used to describe anything horse-related. Most of the horses that exist today are domesticated—that means they are trained to obey humans and do certain things like jump fences or trot. But there are some horses that still roam around in the wild.

Horses are well known for one thing: running super fast! That's why horse racing is a popular cultural pastime and sport. In fact, horse racing dates all the way back to ancient Greek, Egyptian, and Roman times.

FUN FACT: The most popular sport in Rome was chariot racing, in which chariots were pulled by several horses. This was so popular that they built a stadium big enough to hold 350,000 people!

Two of the most famous racing horses of the twentieth century were actually related! At a time when horse racing wasn't well looked upon, **Man o' War** came onto the scene and lifted everyone's spirits. Born in 1917, Man o' War only raced for two years, but in that time he won twenty out of twenty-one races! He

© Pix Inc./The LIFE Picture Collection/Getty Images

was considered a hero when he stopped competing.

Years later, around 1933, the grandson of Man o' War was born. And this horse, named **Seabiscuit**, began wowing crowds just like his granddad did. Although Seabiscuit started off as a disappointing horse in his first years of racing, after a change of owners and trainers, he went on to win eleven of fifteen races in 1937. At the end of his career, Seabiscuit had won thirty-three races in total. He started as an underdog and became known as a true comeback story on the racing scene!

Five Steps to Starting Your Own Garden

♥ ✳ 🦋 ✳ ♥

Have you ever thought about growing your own food? There's nothing quite like nurturing a plant and watching it create food just for you and your friends! Eating organic foods—produced without chemicals or pesticides—is really healthy. It's easy (and natural!) to grow delicious fruits and veggies right in your backyard—just follow these tips! (Don't forget to ask your parents first!)

1. Pick a spot for your garden and prepare the soil. Make sure your soil has plenty of "humus," or organic matter. Mix in compost, leaves, grass, and organic manure. (Make sure the manure is composted too.)

2. Go to your local farmer's market or nursery and pick the seeds and/or plants you want to grow in your garden. A good way to choose? Pick the plants you love to eat! (If you want to stay organic, make sure to ask for plants raised without chemicals.)

3. Plant your seeds and/or plants in wide beds that are roped off so no one can walk on them. Be careful not to plant your seeds too close to one another…you don't want them to overcrowd and not get enough air and light.

4. Water your garden. Try to water as close to the roots as possible, and if you can, water in the morning as opposed to the evening. This gives the plants time to dry off from the sun during the day. (If they stay damp overnight, you risk fungal growths. Yuck!)

5. Weed your garden regularly and apply mulch to the soil to try to lessen the number of weeds that grow.

6. After your plants begin to bear fruit or veggies, wait until the produce Is "rIpe" or ready to be eaten. Share with your family and friends!

Keeping a garden is hard work, but the second you bite into that juicy, ripe organic tomato or strawberry, it will all be worth it. You can even start a community garden with your friends and take turns doing the work. This way, everyone wins!

The Easter Egg Hunt!

EASTER IS JUST AROUND THE CORNER, AND EMMA HAS PREPARED EVERYTHING IN HER GARDEN FOR AN EASTER CELEBRATION WITH HER FRIENDS.

The eggs are hidden, the table is set. Now the guests can come!

Emma, how beautifully you've decorated the garden!

You always go to so much trouble!

We've brought you something.

Oh, thank you!

And I've brought Jazz along! You just can't have Easter without a bunny!

Go, Jazz! Find the eggs!

Hop! Hop!

Well, in that case, the Easter egg hunt can begin!